Pocket Theology
Getting God

T.K. ANDERSON

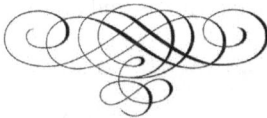

NIA BOOKS
Scottsdale, Arizona

NIA BOOKS
Published by Amazon Createspace
Scottsdale, Arizona (USA)

In Partnership With:
The Social Media Church (TSMchurch.com)
The National Institute of Apologetics (NIAonline.net)

First edition hardcover: September 2017
First edition eBook: July 2017

ISBN: 978-0-692-91457-1

Printed in the United States of America

Dedication

To my wife Dee, who is an amazing example of Christ's love and a far better model of God's relational connectivity than I.

To our children Alyssa, Caite, and Carson. May you always continue to pursue Christ with your whole heart, and may the Lord continually shine His favor upon your lives.

Proverbs 3:5-6

"Trust in the Lord with all your heart,
and do not lean on your own understanding.
In all your ways acknowledge him,
and he will make straight your paths."

CONTENTS

Introduction

Through numerous statistical studies, polling data, and personal conversations, it is, at least to me, abundantly clear the vast majority of humanity has a belief in God. The challenge for us as humans is not in believing but rather in sifting through the many opinions about who God is.

In this easily sized theological volume, I attempt to share some of the most important and very deep doctrinal insights from the Bible, and other well-respected Christian thinkers, at the common level. I do so with the hope of helping the reader to find a better and clearer picture of our Creator without the technical jargon that so often comes with the territory.

I lean heavily upon the penetrating writings of a 19th century theologian, William G. T. Shedd. I enjoy his writing style and straightforward approach to the study of God, and how he implements Scripture toward the aim of a balanced and conservative theology that aligns with historical Christian doctrine dating back to first century core theology.

Through the centuries and myriad of theological opinions, coupled with an insurgence of information readily available from any and all sources, it is easy for modern-day believers to stray off course from the foundational truths. Hopefully, this work will be of help, and will serve as a simple and easy resource for you the reader, to gain a better understanding of God and His purpose for your life. We serve a great and loving God who is passionate about His creation, namely us. May God richly bless you as you learn more about Him, His ways, and His purpose.

T.K. Anderson, 2017
Pastor, The Social Media Church
TSMchurch.com

CHAPTER ONE

Theological ABC's

The Need for Theology

In our current world of varied opinions, alternative facts, and fake news, the need for a coherent and consistent perspective becomes increasingly important especially as one's personal perspective zeros in on the idea and concept of God. Simply put, "Theology (*theou logos*) is the science of God."[1] Thomas Aquinas wrote, "Theology is taught by God, teaches of God, and leads to God."[2] As such, it becomes incumbent upon the believer to embrace a developed system of belief, originating directly from the Scriptures, that is both coherent and truthful.

---

[1] William G.T. Shedd, *Dogmatic Theology*, (Phillipsburg, NJ: Reformed Publishing Company, 2003), 52.
[2] Kevin Alan Lewis, *Prolegomena*, (La Mirada, CA: Biola University, 2017), 1.

Connects us to God

The need for a wide-ranging and thorough study of God is clear. Having this understanding of God connects us to our relationship with Him and is especially co-joined to salvation and our unity within the Body of Christ. John wrote in his gospel, *"Now this is eternal life: that they know you, the only true God, and Jesus Christ, whom you have sent."*[3] Paul declared that Christ gave himself "to equip his people for works of service, so that the body of Christ may be built up until we all reach unity in the faith and in the knowledge of the Son of God and become mature, attaining to the whole measure of the fullness of Christ."[4] From Scripture, we find the necessity to develop a reasoned perspective of God and our relationship to Him, for our personal salvation and our unity with other believers.

Protects us from Error

A secondary and likewise necessity for good theology is to protect our spiritual judgment and belief from improper biblical teaching that expresses

---

[3] John 17:3, NIV
[4] Ephesians 4:12-13, NIV

itself through incongruent views or heresy. By heresy I mean, teachings expressly in contradiction with known biblical truth that run the risk of invalidating one's salvation provided through the substitutionary work of Christ on the cross. It is the responsibility of the theologian and apologist to rightly point to the errors of improper teaching and expose those who attempt to lead followers of Christ astray (II Timothy 4:1-8).

One advantage of solid theological thought is the ease at which erroneous teachings are exposed when compared to the truth. However, when we fail to have "a comprehensive, systematic approach to doctrine," it "places the Christian apologist and polemicist at a disadvantage."[5] Knowing this, we are to be ready to defend the gospel of grace and uphold the biblical doctrines through the aid of good theology.

Our Source of Knowledge

Lastly, it is important to note that Christian theology differs from other branches of knowledge in

---

[5] Kevin Alan Lewis, *Prolegomena*, (La Mirada, CA: Biola University, 2017), 3.

that our source of knowledge is based exclusively upon Scripture. Proper theology, therefore, does not begin with philosophy or other man-made systems of knowledge but rather upon revelation from the Bible. It is the business of the theologian to rightly exegete or "*pull from*" the Scriptures the meaning divinely placed there by God. Once this first step has been accomplished, the theologian utilizes the companion of reason to justify and defend his exegetical study. From this, the dogma and doctrines of theology are refined, sharpened, and employed.

* * * * *

Forms of Theology

The next step in our conversation is to take a glance at the different forms or types of theology. Simply put, there are various categories of theology such as Soteriology (salvation), Christology (all studies related to Christ), Eschatology (the study of end times and future kingdoms), Natural, Historical, Anthropology (man), Bibliology, and others, but the higher categories, if you will, many times take the form of Biblical, Systematic, or Polemical in nature.

It is important to note, within the nature of these forms, the concepts and workings of an individual's worldview are quickly unearthed.

Most simply expressed, "a worldview is a set of presuppositions that one holds, consciously or unconsciously, concerning the essential composition of the world."[6] As the analogous microscope stares inward, we are pressed with the concepts of God, ultimate reality, knowledge, and morality; and eventually, our humanness is discovered as encompassed in and through these thoughts. The pressing questions of the nature of being, and what exactly it means to be human, rest here. Do we have souls? If so, are those souls eternal? Or, are we just material beings and consequently, all meaning is imagined? Thankfully, good theology comes to the aid of these most deeply and perplexing of human questions.

Biblical Theology

This is the technique of developing sound Christian thinking from a particular section or

---

[6] Kevin Alan Lewis, *Prolegomena*, (La Mirada, CA: Biola University, 2017), 7.

division of the biblical texts. For instance, biblical theology focuses on the O.T. at the exclusion of the N.T. or the Pauline epistles with a purposeful absence of the Gospels. While this may be a fair system, to uncover from Scripture the unyielding questions above, this methodology is hampered with a penchant for error. It can be quite easy for a theologian to insert his or her personal ideologies while ignoring important or significant portions of other biblical texts. This thus results in a doctrine that can contradict other more fully established doctrines resting on the totality of Scripture. For this reason, although personal ideologies are not always with intent, many theologians favor using this technique as a support or feeder into the larger and broader form of an unyielding and full-bodied systematic theology.

Systematic Theology

A great example of biblical and systematic theology joining is Calvin's *Institutes*. His systematic approach "is exclusively biblical in its constituent elements and substance. Calvin borrows hardly anything from human philosophy, science, or literature. His appeal is made continually to the

Scripture alone."[7] Theology maintains a status of being a science on account of its dependence on this form. Shedd writes, "Science is a survey of the whole, not of a part. True theological science is to be found in the long series of dogmatic systems extending from Augustine's *City of God* to the present day."[8]

It is also essential to note that because theology is interested in uncovering the whole of the nature of God, Man, Salvation, and more, it is counterproductive to that goal by creating meaning apart from the knowledge base of Scripture and devoid of a larger system or form encompassing the full weight of the matter. This is why the theologian embraces the larger, orderly, logical, and full-bodied form of systematic theology while seeking answers to the unrelenting subjects mentioned above.

Polemical Theology

Once the difficult work of systemizing has been complete, the polemical form of theology comes to

---

[7] William G.T. Shedd, *Dogmatic Theology*, (Phillipsburg, NJ: Reformed Publishing Company, 2003), 48.
[8] Ibid, 49.

the defense of those doctrines. Shedd writes, "From the Greek word *polemos* (war), polemical theology is that branch of theology that attacks other theological positions."[9] Since theology has the aim of uncovering and revealing the truth, this form of theology aids in that goal by removing misunderstanding and false doctrine.

Reason is the friend of this form in that reason does not carry the liability of the revelation concerning the doctrine, yet reason can support and reveal the coherent nature of the doctrine. For instance, reason does not dictate the revelation of the resurrection of Jesus, yet reason can be utilized to dispel falsities of arguments attempting to discredit the biblical account and defend its rationality.

The three-pronged obligation of this form is "1) defending the doctrines, 2) rebutting objections to the doctrines, and 3) showing their consistency with reason."[10] Lastly, it is important to note that the within this form of theology, it is proper and prudent

---

[9] Ibid, 50.
[10] Kevin Alan Lewis, *Prolegomena*, (La Mirada, CA: Biola University, 2017), 3.

for the theologian to utilize extra-biblical sources and ideas when necessary.

* * * * *

Why Skeptics Fall Short

In calling theology the science of God, we do not mean to imply one can obtain all or complete knowledge of God regarding His character and actions. If we were to comprehend all the nature and actions of God, we would either possess omniscience or be God ourselves. Since there is no need to convince any man that he does not possess all knowledge, to me, it seems odd and capricious for man to put forward a cynical view of theology.

The goal of theology is to gain a comprehensive and far-reaching knowledge of God. Because this endeavor, meaning theological studies, contains both the infinite and finite, the journey for this knowledge continues through all generations. Aristotle wrote, "The nature of a thing, is judged by its tendency" (Politics 1.2). The nature of theology is the tendency to seek greater knowledge of God and testing that

19

knowledge through employing reason, debate, and logical systems. It is true to say that good theology is the hard work; conversely, playing the role of the skeptic is the easy bit.

Impossible To Say

John of Damascus (Concerning the Orthodox Faith 3.24) objected, "that theology is not properly speaking the science of God because it is impossible to say what God is."[11] If true, this objection holds all disciplines of human thought and experimentation to provide a complete and full definition of understanding prior to using the label of science in describing said discipline. For example, since there is no true understanding of what or how quantum physics works, it would not qualify as a science under this objection. Yet, one would be hard-pressed to find academia denying the science of quantum physics. In reply to this objection, Thomas Aquinas (Summa 1.1.7) wrote, "If the qualities and relations of an object are the subject matter of any science, it is

---

[11] Ibid, 53.

proper to call it the science of this object."[12] Thus this objection is incorrect since the qualities and relations of God can be studied.

A Superficial View

A second objection is rooted in the charge that theological statements or systems are in contradiction to each other. Skeptics point to doctrines that have been changed or modified over the centuries as proof to self-contradiction or supposed illogical conclusions of theology, proving, therefore, a "superficial view"[13] that is not scientific. Yet these same skeptics seem to forget, in the midst of their harsh judgment, the many times throughout the history of man the self-contradictory claims of other disciplines. Astronomy, for example, stumbled numerous times until the proper understanding was developed and contradictions were removed. The same is true for the fields of medicine, biology, ecology, physics, and such. The old ideas and thoughts are replaced or refined over time after new thoughts, fresh insights, various experimentations,

---

[12] Ibid, 53.
[13] Ibid, 53.

and thoughtful debate are pursued. Thus theology as discussed and researched over time, alongside the Scriptures, strengthens our knowledge of God.

Who's Unscientific?

In truth, the "skeptical estimate of theology is unscientific because it is founded upon a superficial knowledge of the sources and objects of the science."[14] If one is to be, or desires to be, a skeptic of a certain thing, it seems to me a prerequisite of qualifying as said skeptic is to have explanatory knowledge concerning the thing. What often is truthful of skeptics is the surprisingly small base of knowledge concerning theology and the intricacies of the field.

Of the well-known skeptics Hume, Kant, Gibbon, and Froude, it is widely known and freely confessed their lack of knowledge regarding the original manuscripts of Scripture, teachings of the church fathers, or creeds and doctrines developed over the centuries. In comparison to Augustine, Aquinas, Calvin, and Luther, these skeptics are no comparison

---

[14] Ibid, 54.

to the intellectual hard work and dedication to the science of God and His workings within humanity and our world. Most often, we find, with the skeptics, contradictory claims founded upon faulty assumptions and supported by incorrect context.

The driving force behind these erroneous claims is a lack of understanding of the source and object (God) of the science. As Shedd concludes, "The skeptical estimate of Christian theology, consequently, is an unscientific one. Profound and accurate judgment must come from experts. As the scientific comprehension of law is expected from jurists and not from laymen, so that of theology must be sought among philosophers and divines and not among physicists and litterateurs whose studies are devoted to very different branches of knowledge from ethics and theology and who make guerrilla incursions into this field merely for the purpose of attack."[15] The skeptic may be well respected within his field, as he should be. However, if one wishes to branch out into the field of theology, it would be appropriate to spend time doing the hard work,

---

[15] Ibid, 56.

23

alongside those within the field, and from that vantage point, one can offer uncertain views in hopes of better understanding.

T.K. Anderson

CHAPTER TWO

Science and Theology

Is Theology a Science?

We mentioned above, "Theology (*theou logos*) is the science of God."[16] Some may have never heard or thought of theology, which in our cultural language is a '*religious*' base of knowledge, using this type of terminology before. So to them, this concept of theology as being a science, while perhaps welcomed, is new and is in need of further elucidation. While others may feel to call theology a science is to conflate an ethical seeking of knowledge with a concept of obtaining empirical facts and data through experimentation. To be sure, the standard definition of science is, "the state of knowing:

---

[16] William G.T. Shedd, *Dogmatic Theology*, (Phillipsburg, NJ: Reformed Publishing Company, 2003), 52.

knowledge as distinguished from ignorance or misunderstanding."[17]

As a secondary definition, Merriam-Webster continues, "a department of systematized knowledge as an object of study <the *science* of theology>."[18] Although the standard definition of science also includes natural science and the gaining of knowledge through the scientific method focusing exclusively on the physical world, there is no clear elimination of gaining knowledge through other means. We need to pause for a moment to discuss ethics and religion before jumping deeper into this inquiry. These two words are often interchanged with the word *theology*, but to do so is a mistake.

Ethics

It is a mistake to view theology the same as ethics. To do this would be to narrow the expansive size and scope of theology into one segment or channel of the full theological spectrum. One example is the idea of duty, whether that duty is to God or man makes no

---

[17] https://www.merriam-webster.com/dictionary/science, accessed February 4th, 2017.
[18] Ibid, accessed February 4th, 2017.

difference, but that duty is fleshed out in the concept of ethics. Although theology, in part, may contain ethical discussions related to duty, the larger and broader view is one of God's nature, His qualities, His plans, and our relationship to Him. Therefore, ethics is a part of theology, but theology is not contained by ethics.

Although it is important to point out, "ethics is affected by Christian theology, so that Christian ethics differs greatly from pagan ethics. It is more comprehensive because pagan ethics is confined to duties between man and man, while Christian ethics embraces duties toward God."[19] Shedd additionally concludes that pagan ethics are driven by fear and bound by laws made by man, while Christian ethics are bound by the nature and character of God and driven by love.

Religion

It is an additional mistake to view theology the same as religion. In religion, the focus is the

---

[19] William G.T. Shedd, *Dogmatic Theology*, (Phillipsburg, NJ: Reformed Publishing Company, 2003), 51.

worshipper's reverence toward God, acts of service for God, and meditation upon divine things. Cicero, the Roman philosopher, wrote, "Those who diligently observed and repeated, as it were, everything having to do with the worship of gods were called 'religious,' from the verb *relegere* [to reread or choose again]."[20] Shedd writes, "Religion, strictly, would discuss only the relationship of man to the deity; but theology treats first the deity himself and then inferentially of the relations of the creature to him."[21] In comparison to religion, which primarily focuses on man's relationship to God, theology focuses on God first as the Ultimate Being and is the object and focus of study. In truth, theology contains and supervises religion, but religion does not contain or oversee theology.

*　*　*　*　*

Theology as an Absolute Science

In contrast to the physical sciences, theology can be understood as an absolute science. The physical

---

[20] Ibid, 52.
[21] Ibid, 52.

sciences are relative in the sense that the nature and laws upheld by these disciplines are not necessary for existence. In other words, the known laws of the physical universe might have been something different. This is not to say the current physical laws that govern our universe are not constant and unchanging, but rather to point out that our universe could have been different.

If it were possible that our universe could have been created *ex nihilo* differently, then everything we know about the current physical universe would, therefore, be unique. Therefore, it follows that the laws and constants of this differently created universe could be as well. Because the physical laws could have been different, our current physical laws are not absolute and therefore not here by necessity.

This is a strange perspective indeed for those who hold the physical sciences to be absolute, but when one looks into the logical conclusion of the thought, reason dictates this eventual conclusion. Shedd resolves, "There is no absolute knowledge within this domain because there is no absolute object to be known."[22]

Apart from Human Wisdom

Unlike the physical sciences, theology can be thought of as absolute in its foundation. Shedd gives an example of holiness to explain this idea. He writes, "The word *holy* conveyed the same idea to St. Paul that it would to the seraphim; and it conveys the same idea to us that it did to him. It is erroneous to assert that what man calls righteousness in God might be unrighteousness for the angels; and that what the angels call wickedness in Satan might be moral excellence for man. The ideas are the same in kind in all rational intelligence."[23]

The concepts of truth and eternity are logically necessary. They exist in whole and apart from our wisdom or intellect. We cannot conceive of truth or eternity existing in a relative form. A shadow of this is seen in the similarities we find in mathematics. Regardless of human understanding or reasoning, the

---

[22] Ibid, 68.
[23] Ibid, 58.

sum of the angles in all triangles, by necessity of the object, is 180 degrees. The disciplines of logic, ethics, morality, and mathematics share the same quality of being necessary by nature and rise above mere human understanding. The quality and nature of the object is not contingent upon our created universe. For example, moral or ethical laws are grounded in the character and nature of God. It is the business of theology to explore and unearth the richness of these treasures and in the process gives us a glimpse of the nature of our Creator.

Absolute Reason

An additional thought to consider supporting theology, as an absolute science is reason. We can conceive that it would be incongruent and contradictory for God to create two different kinds of reason. However, Shedd writes, "We can conceive of two different kinds of matter."[24] Where the physical laws and matter could be different in nature, reason cannot. The laws of logic dictate that reason itself is necessary by its nature. Theology explores this necessary condition and grounds reason in the nature

---

[24] Ibid, 61.

of God. Reason dictates that issues like right and wrong are not subjective beings, but rather objective values and duties grounded outside of human reason alone. In other words, it is always wrong to commit a certain act in all cases and in all possible worlds.

Since we can conceive this to be true, by necessity, the rightness of this certain act holds an absolute nature. This absolute nature can only be discovered by reason, which was employed by theology as its servant. This is why we safely conclude theology as an absolute science. Shedd concludes, "Accordingly, the laws of mind have more necessity in them than the laws of material nature have. The laws of thought, as enunciated in logic, are more immutable than physical laws. Logic is *a priori* in its regulative principles."[25]

* * * * *

Theology as a Positive Science

When we say that theology is a positive science, we mean to say there are positive statements and

---

[25] Ibid, 61.

logical conclusions to support the idea of God and His interaction with our world. For example, if we were to say a computer is not a toaster, it would not tell us much about what a computer is other than it does not or perhaps cannot make us toast in the morning. However, if we were to say a computer runs on electricity and consists of multiple circuits made of silicon, it would tell us much more about what a computer actually is. In order to gain the best possible understanding of a thing, it is helpful to postulate positive statements describing such a thing.

Negative Knowledge

Listing or making statements of what a thing *is not* would be considered negative knowledge. Some critics (Hobbes & Huet) hold that theology can only provide us with negative knowledge about God because God is unknowable to the human mind. Therefore, this idea leads us to a conclusion that faith is "blind and (an) ignorant credulity of superstition."[26] When working this ideology to its end, at best, one would find himself as an agnostic. Clearly, this would be of no use to the theist.

---

[26] Ibid, 69.

To counter this view of *negative only* theology, it is the job of good theology to offer positive knowledge concerning God. Having said that, Shedd does comment how negative knowledge can and does help the theologian in protecting from erroneous thoughts. He writes, "After saying that God is immanent in the universe, we may say negatively, in order to guard against a pantheistic interpretation of the term *immanent*, that God is not identical with the universe. And after saying that God is distinct from the world, we may add that He is not separate from it, in order to avoid a deistical interpretation of the term *distinct*."[27]

Positive Knowledge

It is possible to affirm that, "faith is intelligent (and) there is some real and true knowledge of the object of faith, although that object is still a mystery in many respects. Some of its properties and relations are known, but not all of them." [28] It is a true statement that man can conclude, "God is spirit and

---

[27] Ibid, 71.
[28] Ibid, 69.

not matter."[29] From that view, we can resolve that spirit would be immaterial and intelligent while perhaps possessing personal qualities. We can conclude that spirit would, therefore, be "incapable of dissolution by material causes."[30] These deductions are true and real knowledge.

We may need additional philosophical help to conclude a personal quality of God. However, it is not impossible to conclude all of these ideas. Because spirit cannot be dissolved through material causes, we may also resolve that God may possess eternal qualities. These are all positive statements concerning who God is. It is important to note that we do not have to possess all or complete knowledge of an object in order to know something about an object. Our physical world easily stands as a vivid example in support of this particular conclusion.

Elenchus

Paul writes to the Ephesians that faith is a "comprehension" of these and other qualities of God.

---

[29] Ibid, 69.
[30] Ibid, 69.

The writer of Hebrews tells us that faith is "evidence" of the things we cannot see. It is interesting to note the word *elenchus*[31] in this passage carries the idea of a conviction of the mind. Shedd writes, "Christian faith is a rational and confident conviction of the mind."[32] In truth, we may be ignorant in some ways to who God is and how and/or why He acts with His creation. Additionally, we may only know a small part of the immense nature of God, but it does not mean that faith is superstitious, unintelligent, or ignorant. Thus, positive knowledge aids the theologian in crafting a solid and systematic approach to his discipline.

---

[31] *elenchus* = a proving or conviction about
[32] Ibid, 69.

CHAPTER THREE

Qualities & Defense of God

The Nature of God

In thinking about the nature of God, we follow the biblical description found in John 4:24, *"God is Spirit."* It is important to distinguish the difference between understanding God as a spirit or God as Spirit. When Jesus declared, "God is Spirit," He was not equating the divine essence of God as the same essence as man or angels, but rather God was to be understood as Spirit, from which all creation owes its existence. In thinking of this idea of Spirit, we have an understanding of the finite nature of our spirit through self-revelation. Yet we can also speculate and comprehend the idea of an infinite Spirit through comparison.

41

The Scriptures tell us that, "God alone is said to have immortality (1 Timothy 6:16), because immortality is *a parte ante*[33] as well as *a parte post*.[34] His immortality is eternity."[35] It is also necessary to deem that God occupies a transcendent nature that is simultaneously immaterial, formless, and unembodied. God's spirituality, which we know as His divine essence, is a necessary essence. Man, as a contingent being, may be similar in nature to God but we do not possess the same nature in kind. Therefore, we can conclude that the necessary being "has more being than a contingent being."[36] Christian theology separates itself from deism and agnosticism in that God is a person and His nature and attributes are knowable by His creation. Shedd writes, "It is because God is a substance and a person that he can possess and exert attributes."[37]

God's Substantiality

When we look at God's nature and discuss the idea of divine essence, it is important to note that

---

[33] In the direction of what comes before (i.e., looking backward in time)
[34] In the direction of what comes after (i.e., looking forward in time)
[35] Ibid, 153.
[36] Ibid, 155.
[37] William G.T. Shedd, *Dogmatic Theology*, (Phillipsburg, NJ: Reformed Publishing Company, 2003), 157.

essence carries the idea of substance. That which has zero substance would be considered a nonentity. Augustine wrote, "God is a certain substance; for whatever is not a substance is nothing at all. Therefore, to be something is to be a substance."[38] God is not a notion or mental hypothesis of the mind. Unlike mathematics, time, or space, which are not objective entities, God is objective and does possess properties of mind.

Plato (Sophist 247-48) writes, "That which possesses any sort of power to affect another or to be affected by another or that which has the power of doing" is the definition of substance or that of an objective being. God has made His presence known to man through self-revelation, creation, and the incarnation of Christ. God does exert power over His creation in personal ways through an impression upon the soul. God does possess substance, thus contrasting unproven theories or mere concepts of the mind. The Scriptures attribute to God numerous qualities, emotions, feelings, thoughts, and identities. When writers of the Bible do this, they do not intend

---

[38] Ibid, 157.

to attach or say that God, as an infinite and perfect being, is like man, but rather search for terms and analogies by way of example to help man understand God's substance and nature. The biblical writers also attribute to God qualities such as love and wrath. While these human qualities are used to form a useful composition of an unlimited being, we are not to mistake these qualities as being attached to or influenced by the creation. These qualities do however help in understanding the nature, essence, and substance of God.

God's Personality

In speaking of God's personality, we mean to say God is self-conscience and aware of the subject and object of that consciousness. By way of example, man has a similar nature in kind, in that we are aware of our own existence and can reflect upon that awareness. For instance, if I were to look upon a baseball stadium, I would, most likely, begin thinking about the objects regarding baseball. Simultaneously, I would also possess the quality and essence to think about why I am thinking about those particular objects and how those thoughts relate to my internal

44

thought processes. Furthermore, I would also possess the ability to have an awareness of the fact that I am even thinking about these types of things.

By way of contrast, unlike animals, which do possess sentient qualities, man has the ability to be aware that he is thinking about himself in relation to the object outside of himself. For example, if a dog is looking and thinking about his treat, he is not aware of his thoughts about the treat nor is he thinking about why he is thinking about this particular treat instead of a different treat. Yet, man has the ability to contemplate the object outside of him and in the same turn reflect upon his mind that is thinking about that particular object. This is the quality and nature of man and by necessity is the same in kind with God.

God as a necessary and Supreme Being would and does possess self-consciousness greater than man. Shedd writes, "Self-consciousness is (1) the power which a rational spirit or mind has of making itself its own object and (2) of knowing that it has done so."[39] God, as a necessary and Supreme Being, most

---

[39] Ibid, 172.

definitely has the capability and nature to be aware of His own existence and is fully aware that He is aware of that nature. Shedd continues on this thought relating that "Consciousness is dual; self-consciousness is trinal." [40] Because God is independent of the universe, meaning His existence is not contingent upon it nor connected to it, God possesses the quality of a unique personhood. The nature of God then must possess the ability to reflect upon Himself, similar in kind to man, thus leading us to an insight into the personhood of God. Shedd concludes, "The biblical doctrine of three distinctions in one essence, each of which possesses the whole undivided essence, show how God's self-consciousness is independent of the universe. God makes himself his own object."[41]

* * * * *

Innate Knowledge of God

It is possible and very real for man to possess an internal understanding and knowledge of God

---

[40] Ibid, 172.
[41] Ibid, 174.

completely separate from his outward senses, and this thus concludes, God is real. We call this internal understanding innate knowledge. In its opening sentence, the Scriptures affirm, "*In the beginning God created the heaven and the earth.*" It is written with an understanding that man does possess universal knowledge of God's existence.

In fact, the Bible does not generally contest atheism on account of this presupposition of man's internal knowledge of his Creator. Shedd writes, "The only form of atheism combated in the Bible is practical atheism. The 'fool' says there is no God (Psalm 14:1)."[42] Yet here we find an interesting dilemma for the atheist in that man's concept of causation is a most certain fact, however that certainty points man back to God. Nonetheless, we catch the atheist in that he must disavow his intuitive judgment of causation, for if he does not, it then leads him to a first cause.

The biblical writers understood this dilemma and wrote from the perspective of bypassing it altogether.

---

[42] William G.T. Shedd, *Dogmatic Theology*, (Phillipsburg, NJ: Reformed Publishing Company, 2003), 185.

In truth, the understanding of God's existence is more certain than the understanding of causation. The biblical writers took the position that a believer as well as "the pagan possesses a knowledge of God as invisible (*ta aorato autou*), eternal (*aidios dynamis)*, omnipotent, supreme, holy in revealing wrath, against sin, one, and benevolent (Acts 17:25; 14:16; Romans 2:24)."[43]

Pagan Evidence

It is furthermore intriguing to find early pagan writers and philosophers, from ancient times, often speaking of one God through name and religious systems. This further supports the idea of man's innate knowledge of a Supreme Being. Shedd writes, "Cudworth has discussed the heathen theology represented by Greece and Rome with immense learning and great candor. He proves by abundant quotations (1) that many of the pagan philosophers were 'theists,' that is, monotheists, and acknowledged one supreme God; and (2) that the multiplicity of gods, of which they speak, does not denote many eternal and self-existent deities, but

---

[43] Ibid, 186.

only inferior divinities produced by the Supreme Being and subject to him; the word *gods* being employed by them somewhat as it is in Scripture to signify angels, princes and magistrates (Intellectual System 1.370ff., 417ff. [ed. Tegg])." [44]

During the first century B.C., the Roman philosopher Cicero wrote, "There is no animal excepting man that has any notion of God: and among men there is no tribe so uncivilized and savage which, even if it does not know what kind of a god it ought to have, does not know that it ought to have one."[45] DeVere writes (*Studies in English, 10*), "The term for God is identical in all the Indo-European languages—the Indic Iranic, Celtic, Hellenic, Italic, Teutonic, and Sclavonic."[46] Even though man does possess this innate knowledge of God, he is prone to misunderstand this knowledge either for selfish and sinful reasons, or for lack of complete knowledge due to a void of good theology based upon the Scriptures.

---

[44] Ibid, 188.
[45] Ibid, 188.
[46] Ibid, 188.

Shedd clarifies this point by writing, "According to John 1:4 there is a natural apprehension of God; and according to 1:5 there is a sinful misapprehension of him. The Logos was 'the light of men,' and 'the darkness comprehended not' this light. The first statement relates to the innate idea of God given by creation; the second, to the innate idea as vitiated by sin."[47] St. Paul, in his writings, held that man is ultimately responsible for this innate knowledge and that we all will give answer, or account, for what we have done with it.

* * * * *

Arguments for the Divine Existence

Like a four-bladed propeller on a ship, four main philosophical arguments serve to drive belief in God forward. These arguments are not offered in an attempt to prove the claims of the Christian God *a priori*, but rather to establish the existence of God in general.

The Ontological Argument

The Ontological argument for God's existence

---

[47] Ibid, 189.

"claims that proper reasoning about the idea of a Perfect Being generates the conclusion that God exists."[48] This argument holds that God's existence is logical and necessarily holds true with zero reliance upon disputable empirical conditions. This argument is credited to St. Anselm (c. 1033-1109). In chapter three of *Proslogium,* Anselm writes, "God cannot be conceived not to exist. God is that, than which nothing greater can be conceived. That which can be conceived not to exist is not God."[49] From this thought, it follows that God is the type of being that possesses necessary existence, meaning "God exists as a matter of logical necessity. God does not exist as a contingent state of affairs."[50] As a necessary being, God would possess numerous qualities.

The Cosmological Argument

The Cosmological Argument finds its potency in the concept of the universe owing its existence to something outside itself. This dependency on an outside source is found in both the creation of the

---

[48] Ibid, 185.
[49] Anselm, *Proslogium 3*, accessed Dec. 2, 2016,
http://sourcebooks.fordham.edu/halsall/basis/anselm-
proslogium.asp#CHAPTER%20III
[50] Groothuis, *Christian Apologetics A Comprehensive Case for Biblical Faith*, 195.

universe and the sustaining force of its current existence. These concepts truly come to a tipping point with the question, "why is there something rather than nothing?" Philosophers across the ages (Kant, Russell, Leibniz, Heidegger, and Craig) have written widely concerning this question.

The first premise states, "Whatever begins to exist has a cause." From there, Craig points out, "The universe began to exist. Therefore, the universe has a cause and the cause of the universe is God."[51] It all begins with the first premise, "ex nihilo nihil fit" ('out of nothing, nothing comes').[52] If the critic wishes to argue otherwise, he needs to show clear and convincing proof, both philosophically and scientifically, that material matter can simply pop into existence from nothing.

We can suppose this is a burden too large to bear upon sound logic and scientific observation of how our universe works. It seems to me it is illogical at best, and irresponsible at least, to affirm, as Russell

---

[51] Ibid, 214.
[52] Ibid, 215.

did, "The universe was 'just there' and in need of no explanation."[53] Although, if that is the course a critic wishes to take, even the Naturalist David Hume is waiting with a reply: "allow me to tell you that I never asserted so absurd a Proposition as *that anything might arise without a cause.*"[54] It is logical and coherent to conclude that nothing creates nothing and sustains nothing. Therefore, if the universe is a something, then something or someone is the cause.

The Moral Argument

The Moral Argument for God's existence is by far the most humanly intuitive and easily accessible argument to understand. For example, moral outrage within the human experience is undoubtedly real and widely experienced. We often find ourselves making statements and giving direction to other people, utilizing words like *you ought*, *you should*, or *you must*. But where do we get this sense of commanding people they *ought*, *should*, or *must* do anything? Furthermore, where does this authority to command anyone or anything come from? Moreover, why do

---

[53] Ibid, 211.
[54] David Hume, *"To John Stewart," Letter 91*, ed. J.Y.T. Greig (Oxford, Eng: Clarendon, 1932), 1:187.

we experience a personal sense of outrage, offense, or anger when we hear of or see child abuse, social injustice, or genocide?

Somehow, we conclude internally that there is something *just not right* about these situations and we have a *duty* to stop certain despicable deeds. It seems to me that this type of moral outrage and moral intuition points an arrow in the direction of objective moral values and duties. This, in turn, raises the question of where these objective values and duties come from. From a Theistic point of view, we hold that objective moral values are centered on the personhood and character of God, meaning, goodness is right because God is good and love is superior to hate because God is love. Simply put, God is the moral authority.

The Design (Teleological) Argument

The Design Argument (DA) supports the view that our universe has been finely tuned for our existence. This argument raises the question, "if we see design, is there a designer?" From a Theistic perspective, we affirm, "that the universe is the handiwork of a designing agent. The Creator brought everything into existence *ex nihilo* and engineered the structure and function of the universe.[55] For example, if we were to compare the Grand Canyon to Mount Rushmore, it would be easy to conclude natural forces created the former while a designer created the latter. It is important also to note that the DA looks beyond random chance and apparent design in the universe.

In truth, there are wonders within our universe that appear designed, but under further inquiry, we discover natural laws plus time created the illusion of design. This has brought some to conclude along with "choruses of secular voices, many of whom shout loudly from the scientific academy . . . that humans and the rest of the cosmos are nothing but the result of time, space, matter/energy, impersonal laws and chance."[56] However, this chorus of scientific and philosophical vocalists was challenged when "one of the twentieth century's leading atheist philosophers," Antony Flew "renounced atheism in 2007 on the

---

[55] Ibid, 344.
[56] Ibid, 240.

basis of the evidence for a Designer and a Creator."
Flew was clear in his bestselling book *There is a God*
that he endeavored to "follow the argument wherever
it leads."[57] As he followed the evidence for design, he
landed upon the belief in a designer.

It is reasonable to conclude, the design of universe
is not contingent upon any known natural laws.
Suppose you flew to Mars, and when you arrived,
you noticed a huge biosphere. In the facility was
everything you and your party needed to survive and
flourish. In the control room, you noticed a series of
dials and levers that controlled all the necessary
functions that made life for you possible on Mars;
atmospheric buttons, biological measurements, plate
tectonics controls, oxygenation quantities, and a
myriad of other fine-tuned metrics that if off
by .0000000000000000001% in any direction would
mean certain death for you and your party. In other
words, you noticed a very distinct bubble that was
fine-tuned for your existence. Would it be reasonable
to conclude that perhaps a designer designed this

---

[57] Antony Flew with Ray Abraham Varghese, *There Is a God* (San Francisco, CA: HarperOne, 2007), 88.

bubble? Of course, it would. In truth, for you to conclude it was by chance or natural law would be irrational. If we take the bubble of Mars and simply expand it out to include the bubble of our universe, it seems reasonable to conclude that our universe contains the specificity needed to check the box for a designer.

Quick Summary

The Ontological argument shows that God is the type of being that possesses necessary existence. The Cosmological argument reveals the universe owing its existence to something outside itself. The Moral argument holds that objective moral laws do exist and objective moral laws must have a moral lawgiver. The Design argument shows that our universe has been finely tuned for our existence.

CHAPTER FOUR

God's Characteristics

Divine Attributes – Aseity & Platonism

Central to the Christian faith is the concept of God existing *a se* from the Latin meaning "by itself." Aseity, in referring to God, is the quality of God's self-existence or complete independence of or with anything else. The theist holds, God is the greatest possible being and would exist in all possible worlds with or without anything, solely alone, and complete. As simple as this sounds, there have been many challenges and critiques over the centuries to the idea of divine aseity in referring to God. The most ardent and longstanding challenger facing the theist finds its foundational concepts forged in the debates of ancient Greek philosophy.

59

Platonism

Platonism is a philosophical viewpoint, which holds that alongside physical and concrete objects such as people, planets, and parking lots, there also exist invisible, abstract objects like numbers, properties, and propositions. This poses a major problem for a theistic worldview in that if abstract objects exist *a se,* as God does, it challenges the very idea of God's uniqueness and he becomes infinitesimal and somewhat irrelevant among a myriad of other abstract objects.

This ancient Greek philosophy finds its roots in none other than Plato himself. Although the point of view discussed in this post will lean toward a more present-day view of this philosophical ideology, the foundations extend backward in time over two thousand years. Platonism "is the view that there exist such things as abstract objects — where an abstract object is an object that does not exist in space or time and which is therefore entirely non-physical and non-mental. Platonism in this sense is a *contemporary* view. It is obviously related to the views of Plato in significant ways, but it is not entirely evident that Plato endorsed this view."[58]

Every Possible World

To develop this philosophy further, these abstract objects exist necessarily, meaning there would be no possible world in which these objects would not exist. J.P. Moreland writes, "It is inconceivable that there should exist, for example, a possible world lacking in numbers or propositions, even if that world were altogether devoid of concrete objects other than God himself." [59] In Platonism, the undeniable conclusion is that abstract objects exist *a se*, which brings an unsettling problem to the theist's position. There is no cause for these objects. The sheer size and scope of all possible abstract objects are mind bending as well. There exist infinities of sets and numbers alone. In a sense, "God finds himself amid uncreated, infinite realms of beings that exist just as necessarily and independently as he."[60] Some theists do not accept the view of Platonism and argue against

---

[58]Platonism in Metaphysics (revision Tue Apr. 7, 2009)
http://plato.stanford.edu/entries/platonism/#5, accessed May 10, 2015
[59] J.P. Moreland & William Lane Craig, *Philosophical Foundations for a Christian Worldview* (Downers Grove, Il: InterVarsity Press, 2003), 504.
[60] Ibid, 504.

its perspective. These thinkers find the idea of God and abstract objects existing together *a se* undermining to the doctrine of creation *ex nihilo*, creation out of nothing.

William Lane Craig writes, "God alone exists *a se*; all else exists *ab alio* and is, therefore, dependent upon God for its existence. This is a core tenet of the doctrine of God, one grounded in Scripture and tradition. If Platonism is true, then, there literally is no God."[61] Craig has a valid point in that Scripture teaches very strongly God is the Creator of all things and before Him, there was nothing.

All Things Through Him

There is strong biblical support for Craig's observation, and clearly, the beginning of the Gospel of John upholds the idea of God's unique status as the sole and final authority. John writes,

> In the beginning was the Word, and the Word was with God, and the Word was God. He was in the beginning with God. All things

---

[61] William Lane Craig, "A Nominalist Perspective on God and Abstract Objects," *Philosophia Christi* 13 (2011): 305.

came into being through him, and without him not one thing came into being. What has come into being in him was life, and the life was the light of all people. The light shines in the darkness, and the darkness did not overcome it.[62]

Craig points out in his lecture on the *Coherence of Theism* that John was most familiar at the time with the teaching of Greek philosophy and would have intended to include "all things" within the words that through the "Word" **Logos**, "all things came into being." Additionally, Craig points to the teachings of the early church fathers to support the view that Platonism is contrary to early church doctrine. In fact, the Nicene Creed affirms;

> I believe in one God, the Father, Almighty, Maker of heaven and earth and of all things visible and invisible;
>
> And in one Lord, Jesus Christ, the only Son of God, begotten of the Father before all ages, light from light, true God from true God, begotten not made, consubstantial with

---

[62] The Holy Bible, *Gospel of John Chapter 1:1-5* (New Revised Standard Version, 1989)

the Father, through whom all things came into being.

Craig explains, "The phrase 'Maker of heaven and earth and of all things visible and invisible' derives from Paul and the expression 'through whom all things came into being' from the prolog to John's Gospel. The Council affirms that everything other than God was created by God through the Son, so that God alone is uncreated."[63]

* * * * *

Natural Divine Attributes

Divine attributes associated with God's essence and nature can be divided into many categories. At times, these categories are a source of debate among theologians. It is important to note however, no matter the methodology of categorization, divine attributes are not merely subjective thoughts of man, but rather the objective reality of God's nature. Two general categories include natural and moral attributes. The following five attributes are

[63] William Lane Craig, Coherence of Theism Conference (Marietta, GA: Biola University, April 17-18, 2015)

considered to be natural attributes. These attributes are an expected part of God's substance and nature.

Simplicity

This attribute connotes God as undividable, uncomplicated, and unattached to anything other than Himself. God is not a sum of many parts or a collection of different essences. He is one in being. His essence is of one substance, unembodied, and unconnected to the external world. Unlike man who is complex with a body and soul, two substances, God is one in substance. Unlike the universe that is contingent, complex, and designed with many parts, God is non-contingent, simple, and outside of the physical universe as Paul wrote in Romans 11:36, "All things are of him (*ex autou*)."

Infinity

God is said to be infinite, meaning, without boundaries or maximums. There is no such thing as lack of knowledge with God. There is no such thing as lack of power with God. God is beyond, independent of, or unconnected to time and His nature is eternal. Time has no hold upon God's being. It is accurate to say God created and governs time.

God knows no limits to His abilities, knowledge, or nature. If God did have limits, that would infer imperfection. For example, lack of knowledge constitutes imperfect knowledge. God, by nature of being perfect, cannot possess any imperfection. Therefore, we say as Shedd writes, God is "perfect in every respect in which he is infinite."[64]

Immensity and Omnipresence

When we speak of God's omnipresence, we are relating God's essence and nature to space. Because God is Spirit, He does not possess an "extension of substance."[65] God's nature is unable to be measured, "The heavens cannot contain you"[66] pronounce the writers of Scripture. Because God possesses the quality and nature of immensity, by nature, He additionally possesses the attribute of omnipresence. Shedd writes, "Immensity and omnipresence are thus inseparably connected and are best considered in reference to each other. Omnipresence has respect to the universe of created beings and things – to space

---

[64] William G.T. Shedd, *Dogmatic Theology*, (Phillipsburg, NJ: Reformed Publishing Company, 2003), 277.
[65] Ibid, 277.
[66] Ibid, 277.

as filled. Immensity has reference to this and to what is beyond – to space as void. God is said to be beyond the universe (*extra mundum*)."[67] In relation to all things, God is not present to all things, but rather all things are present to God.

Eternity

When we speak of God's nature possessing eternity, we are referring to duration. Because God is eternal, He has no beginning or end. It is important to note that eternity is different from immortality. Man, through Christ, acquires the quality and potential to gain immortality. However, this implies a beginning to each man. God does not possess a beginning; therefore, we say God is eternal instead. There is no *before* or *after* concerning God and His essence. Aquinas writes (*Summa* 1.10.4), "Eternity is complete all at once, but in time there is 'before' and 'after.' Therefore time and eternity are not the same thing."[68] In Isaiah 46:10, God "declares the end from the beginning." God does not have succession of thought. He sees all things concurrently.

---

[67] Ibid, 277.
[68] Ibid, 279.

Immutability

This natural attribute is in reference to the unchangeableness of God's essence. Since God's knowledge lacks nothing, His knowledge will never change. There is no adding to God's knowledge or taking away from it. The same is true regarding God's presence and God's experience. Shedd writes, "Immutability results from eternity, as omnipresence does from immensity."[69] Since God also does not possess the idea or concept of succession, He can therefore be the same, "yesterday, today, and forever: 'I am Jehovah, I change not' (Malachi 3:6)."[70]

It is noteworthy to point out that God cannot have or acquire new attributes at a later time. He is perfect in being and lacks nothing. The attribute of immutability additionally applies to His divine will, also known as His divine decrees. It is therefore safe to conclude that God does not change His mind or His will. Shedd explains this point, saying, "It is one thing for God to will a change in created things external to himself and another thing for him to change in his own nature and character. God can will

---

[69] Ibid, 284.
[70] Ibid, 284.

a change in the affairs of men ... and yet his own will remain immutable, because he had from eternity willed and decreed that change."[71]

* * * * *

More Natural & Moral Divine Attributes

Omniscience – a natural attribute

This natural attribute communicates that God possesses all knowledge. God knows all things that are and all things that are possible. There is no thing that is possible or actual that God is not aware of and possesses no knowledge of. To man, God's knowledge may seem like foreknowledge, but to God, who possesses no before or after, all knowledge is expressed in simple knowledge without succession. Divine knowledge is intuitive, simultaneous, and complete. Shedd writes, "Divine knowledge excludes knowledge by the senses, gradual acquisition of knowledge, forgetting of knowledge, and recollection of knowledge." [72] Charnock writes (*God's Knowledge*), "What is foreknowledge but the

---

[71] Ibid, 285.
[72] William G.T. Shedd, *Dogmatic Theology*, (Phillipsburg, NJ: Reformed Publishing Company, 2003), 286.

knowledge of the future. But what is future to God? For, if divine knowledge includes all things at one instant, all things are present to him, and there is nothing future; and his knowledge is knowledge and not foreknowledge."

Omnipotence – a natural attribute

God is said to possess absolute power, meaning, anything does not limit Him or any source cannot make Him unable to accomplish His divine will. God's power is made manifest in creation, in providence, and in redemption. It is also important to point out that God cannot "do anything inconsistent with the perfection of divine nature."[73] Hebrews 6:18 says, "*It is impossible for God to lie.*" 2 Timothy 2:13 attests, "*He cannot deny himself.*" James 1:13 says, "*God cannot be tempted.*" We can also say that God cannot make a square triangle or married bachelor. Shedd concludes, "Divine power is limited only by the absurd and self-contradictory. God can do anything that does not imply a logical impossibility. A logical impossibility means that the predicate is contradictory to the subject."[74]

---

[73] Ibid, 289.
[74] Ibid, 289.

Holiness – a moral attribute

This moral attribute of God's essence is in relation to Himself. God is holy by nature, meaning, His is right. God is the standard by which all things are measured. There is absolutely, by necessity, no wrongness in His character. In fact, wrongness is only characterized and deemed as such in comparison to God's divine nature. His is the standard, from which all things derive rightness. There is no thing or no action possessing the quality of rightness that would not and does not find its origin within God's divine essence.

This is in contradistinction to man's holiness. When we think of man's relation to holiness, we think of our rightness or wrongness of actions and intention of the heart in comparison to a measure or standard outside of ourselves. How do we measure up to that standard? God does not do this, for He is the standard.

1 Peter 1:14-16,

> *As obedient children, do not be conformed to the passions of your former ignorance, but as*

71

> *he who called you is holy, you also be holy in*
> *all your conduct, since it is written, "You*
> *shall be holy, for I am holy."*

Goodness (Including Benevolence and Mercy) – a moral attribute

God is good in His divine nature. From that goodness, He bestows benevolence and mercy to His creatures. Benevolence and mercy do not make God good. Because God is good, these qualities flow naturally as moral attributes of the divine essence. God cares for His creation in a personal sense and His care extends to man even in sinful form. This care "grows out of the fact that the creature is his workmanship. God is interested in everything which he has made."[75] Divine benevolence knows no limits and can be bestowed by God upon His creation freely.

Mercy is a second quality of divine goodness. God shows His mercy to sinful man even though we may reject God's benevolence. From mercy, God additionally shows grace to mankind. Shedd writes,

---

[75] Ibid, 304.

"Grace is an aspect of mercy. It differs from mercy in that it has reference to sinful man as guilty, while mercy has respect to sinful man as miserable."[76] Romans 9:15 states, *"I will have mercy on whom I will have mercy, and I will have compassion on whom I have compassion."*

Truth – a moral attribute

As a part of God's divine essence, God is incapable to not fulfill what He said he would do. Jesus declared in John 14:6, *"I am the way, and the truth, and the life."* We know from this divine testimony that truth is not a concept, ideology, or philosophy, but rather truth is a person. God is truth and from Him, all truth flows. God's attribute of truth is revealed in (1) revelation, (2) redemption, and (3) retribution toward sin.

God's revelation to man through the Scriptures, the incarnation, and personal experience points to God's truthfulness in revealing His nature and personage to man. Concerning redemption, because God is truthful, His word is true. Paul writes in

---

[76] Ibid, 307.

Romans 10:13, *"Everyone who calls on the name of the Lord will be saved."* Lastly, in terms of retribution, God will judge those who choose not to accept the free gift of salvation found in Jesus Christ. God's divine essence cannot allow ultimate judgment to be stayed or passed over to either the sinner or the agent of substitution. In the case of the Christian, through God's divine attribute of goodness, Jesus Christ is the atonement for sin.

CHAPTER FIVE

The Triune Portrait

Of God

The Trinity: Scripture, Essence, Persons

Scriptural Evidence

It is correct to say our understanding of the Trinity, implied to be the triune nature of God, is a revelation to man, which comes from the direct study of Scripture. There is no single passage or verse that utilizes the name *Trinity*, however, one can easily understand through proper study, the classical understanding of God's one essence consisting of three distinct personhoods. Shedd offers a further explanation by writing, "The term *person* does not denote an attribute of the essence, but a mode of the essence. That is, a particular form of its existence, according to the term used by St. Paul in Philippians 2:6. It is proper to speak of a Trinitarian mode, but not of a Trinitarian attribute."[77] There are two typical classes of writings that describe God's nature as three in one. One set of biblical writings describes all "three persons of the Godhead."[78] Another set of biblical writings "teach the deity of one or another of the persons singly."[79]

New Testament

Let us take a look at the first set of biblical writings. At the beginning of Jesus' earthly ministry, the baptism of Christ references three persons in Matthew 3:16-17. The Father from heaven speaks concerning the Son and a descending dove represents the Holy Spirit. At the conclusion of His earthly ministry, Jesus gives His followers instructions to administer baptisms in the name of "the Father and of the Son and of the Holy Spirit" in Matthew 28:19. It is important to note Jesus spells out no distinction in

---

[77] William G.T. Shedd, *Dogmatic Theology*, (Phillipsburg, NJ: Reformed Publishing Company, 2003), 229.
[78] Ibid, 224.
[79] Ibid, 224.

this passage. He says, "...in the name..." not "in the *names*," meaning God is one, though manifesting Himself in three personhoods.

The implication points to equal authority among three distinct persons. Additionally, Paul and Peter note all three persons of God's essence in 2 Corinthians 13:14, Ephesians 4:4-6, and 1 Peter 1:2. Moreover, some biblical passages point to specific duties or actions performed by the Father, Son, and Holy Spirit. John 14 & 15 speaks of the Holy Spirit as the Comforter who truthfully testifies concerning the Son and is sent to us by the Son and of the Father.

Old Testament

Some passages in the Old Testament, which reference God as a plurality, indicate the doctrine of the Trinity as well. Shedd writes, "When God himself employs the plural number in speaking of himself and his agency, it evidently supports the doctrine of personal distinctions in the essence: 'God said, let us make man after our image.' (Genesis 1:26)."[80] In Genesis 3:12, the Godhead declares man "became as

---

[80] Ibid, 227.

one of us." In reference to the 'tower of Babel' story, Genesis 11:17 records God as speaking, *"let us go down and there confound their language."* Lastly, Isaiah 7:8 articulates, "Whom shall I send and who will go for us?"

Augustine writes (*City of God* 16.6), "We might have supposed that the words uttered at the creation of man, 'Let us,' not Let me, 'make man,' were addressed to the angels, had he not added, 'in our image'; but as we cannot believe that man was made in the image of the angels or that the image of God is the same as that of angels, it is better to refer this expression to the plurality of the Trinity."[81]

* * * * *

God is One in Respect to Essence

To understand the Trinity, it is important to distinguish the difference between essence and persons. The doctrine of the Trinity carries the proposition that "God is one in respect to essence."[82]

---

[81] Ibid, 227.
[82] William G.T. Shedd, *Dogmatic Theology*, (Phillipsburg, NJ: Reformed Publishing Company, 2003), 230.

We understand essence to be, "the whatness or quiddity of a thing. It is those properties or qualities that make a being or thing precisely what it is, and not something else."[83] In English, we use terms like *essence, substance, nature*, and *being* to describe the 'whatness' of God's existence.

Early Debate

There was early debate between Greek and Latin theologians utilizing the native terms of *ousia* and *essentia/substantia* respectively, due to a confusion of the Latin translation of *substantia* being translated *hypostasis* as well as *ousia* in the Greek. These Greek terms carry the idea of personhood and thus create indistinctness within the language and understanding. It was vital for early theologians to separate the differences between essence/substance and personhood in relation to the doctrine of the Trinity.

Augustine, from the Latin church, wrote (*On the Trinity* 7.4), "That which must be understood of persons, according to our usage, is to be understood

---

[83] Kevin Alan Lewis, *Essential Christian Doctrine Theology Proper II*, (Biola University, 2017), 2.

of substances, according to the Greek usage: for they say three substances (*hypostaseis*), one essence, in the same way as we say three persons, one essence or substance (*essentiam vel substantiam*)."[84] Accurate language was essential to combat the twofold heretical teachings from the Arians "who denied that the Son is from either the Father's essence or the Father's person,"[85] and the Semiarians, "who denied that he is from the Father's essence but conceded that he is from the Father's person."[86]

Simple Form

We say God's essence or nature is eternal and simple. One essence is simple. Three separate persons or three essences are complex and therefore have diverse substances. God is unique in that He has a simple essence yet contains three persons or forms. Shedd writes, "Essence is derived from *esse* (to be) and denotes energetic being."[87] It is important to point out that without the personhood of God, the substance of God would be without personality.

---

[84] Shedd, 231.
[85] Ibid, 231.
[86] Ibid, 231.
[87] Ibid, 232.

A divine nature without personality yields an impersonal deity. Thus the concept of the Tri-unity of God's nature supports the conclusion of "divine self-consciousness."[88] A danger waits for the doctrine of infinite substance void of the doctrine of the Trinity in that infinite substance yields a "deity of pantheism."[89] Just as in man the activities of the mind, body, and spirit show the personality of a man, God's essence through the doctrine of the Trinity shows us divine personality as the Father begets the Son and the Son and Father send the Spirit and the Spirit reveals the Son while the Son glorifies the Father. These divine activities show us a God who is personal as He is shown to be "self-contemplating, self-knowing, self-communing."[90]

* * * * *

God is Three in Respect to Persons

When we say God is three persons, do we mean to say God is three individuals, distinct in essence, form, and function? Partly yes, but only in terms of

---

[88] Ibid, 232.
[89] Ibid, 232.
[90] Ibid, 233.

function not of essence. Do we mean to explain God's personhood as similar to a comparison of three specific individuals such as George Washington, Abraham Lincoln, and Ronald Reagan? No, we are not explaining God in this type of individualistic form or fashion. We mean to say that God is one in essence but has the unique, one of a kind, form of maintaining three personhoods as the Father, Son, and Holy Spirit. God's essence does not change nor is His essence disconnected or separated. He is connected as one in substance but holds three equal subsistence's simultaneously and eternally. Shedd concedes, "This side of the doctrine is the most difficult to apprehend because analogies from the finite are difficult to find and, if found, are exceedingly recondite and abstruse."[91]

God is Spirit

A unique characteristic regarding God's nature is that He is spiritual in substance. As Spirit, His essence has the capability to retain divine form yet exist instantaneously in three distinct forms. In our

---

[91] William G.T. Shedd, *Dogmatic Theology*, (Phillipsburg, NJ: Reformed Publishing Company, 2003), 233.

material world, we have difficulty comprehending this biblical truth due to the fact that material forms or substances are unable to take on three forms simultaneously.

For instance, water does not exist in frozen, liquid, and vaporous forms at the same time. While God can and does exist in multiple forms at the same time, we stretch our minds in attempting to understand this great mystery. Shedd creates two examples to help aid us in understanding God's three-in-one mystery. He writes, "One and the same entire mind may remember, understand, and will simultaneously. Memory, understanding, and will are three simultaneous forms or modes of one and the same mind or spirit. In self-consciousness, also, one and the same mind may be subject, object, and subject-percipients simultaneously."[92]

Help from Scripture

The Scripture teaches of this hypostatic essence concerning the divine nature. Jesus fully recognizes that as the Son, He is separate from the Father, and so

---

[92] Ibid, 235.

He says, *"Father, glorify me in your own presence with the glory that I had with you before the world existed"* (John 17:5). The Father, as well, distinguishes that He and the Son are unique persons, saying, *"You are my Son, today I have begotten you"* (Hebrews 1:5). The Holy Spirit also exhibits a distinct awareness that He is neither the Son nor the Father, when, for example, He commands, *"Set apart for me Barnabas and Saul for the work to which I have called them"* (Acts 13:2).

Augustine further clarifies this extraordinary secret, "Each [person] is in each [person], and all [three persons] are in each [person], and each [person] in is all [three persons], and all [three persons] are one [being]" (*On the Trinity* 6.10). Lastly, it is important to point out there is no greater or lesser in terms of quality, power, or order within the Trinity. The Son is not lesser than the Father and the Spirit is not greater than the Son. There is a perfect equality among the divine persons of the Trinity even though there is a "kind of subordination among them."[93]

---

[93] Ibid, 251.

Flatland and Spaceland

During my graduate work at Biola University, a student named Curt Blattman wrote the following in an attempt to illustrate the difficulty we face attempting to comprehend God as one essence, yet three persons. Curt wrote, "Back in 1884 Edwin Abbott wrote a short book called *Flatland: A Romance of Many Dimensions.* In his book Abbott tells a fascinating story of a Square living in a land called Flatland, a place of only two dimensions. One day the Square is paid a visit from an unexpected visitor called Sphere, who lives in a land called Spaceland, a realm of three dimensions. Square is fascinated by Sphere and believes, that even though he only knows of a two-dimensional world, that there is such a thing as the existence of a third dimension. Square is excited by this new concept and decides to share this fascinating new knowledge with his fellow citizens of Flatland. Rather than believe Square his fellow inhabitants think he is crazy and place him in prison.

"There is an interesting parallel with us, and our attempt to understand the Trinity. We live in a three-

87

dimensional world and we are trying to understand a God and the idea of the Trinity from a God that is not bound by our concept of dimensions. Just as Square cannot understand Sphere we can't fully understand the Trinity because our point of reference is different and limited from God's point of reference. We indeed are fortunate in that God understands our limitations and chose to come into our world of limited dimensions through His Son Jesus and reveal to us some of the mysteries of the Godhead."

CHAPTER SIX

The Divine Decree

Characteristics of the Divine Decree

Grounded in God's Attributes

One important aspect of God's nature and essence is the acting out of His divine attributes through what we call the divine decrees. The divine decrees can best be understood as one all-encompassing decree in sum, as not to confuse the concept of sequential reasoning or thinking within God's triune and eternal nature. This connection between the acting out of attributes through decision-making and foreknowledge is not difficult for us to comprehend. As human beings, we experience a similar relationship in that our actions are tied to our nature.

A man cannot be separated from the connection between his actions and decisions anymore can God

91

be separated in the same manner. Because we say God is eternal and His attributes are divine, it therefore must follow that His decree or decisions are the same in nature and form. Shedd writes, "The actions of God can no more be separated from the decrees of God than the action of a man can be from his decisions. The divine decree relates only to God's *opera ad extra* or transitive acts. It does not include those immanent activities which occur within the essence and result in the three Trinitarian distinctions."[94]

Founded in Eternity

The divine decree is therefore in relation to those things or events that occur with time. In God's mind, because He is omniscience, there is no sequence of time or decision-making, as we understand decision-making. God foreordains that which is to come to pass, inside of our temporal world. It would be proper to say, "The divine decree is formed in eternity, but executed in time. There are sequences in the execution, but not in the formation of God's eternal

---

[94] William G.T. Shedd, *Dogmatic Theology*, (Phillipsburg, NJ: Reformed Publishing Company, 2003), 311.

purpose."[95] We understand this concept from the Scripture as the apostle John wrote, "...the Lamb who was slain from the creation of the world" (Revelation 13:8).

We understand from this verse, there was a sequence of time from the beginning of this temporal universe until the time of Christ's birth. We additionally understand this to include His eventual death and resurrection events as well. Yet, John clearly writes of the personhood of Christ knowing of His ultimate course from the beginning of creation itself. Paul additionally writes on the subject when he remarks, "according to the eternal purpose that he has realized in Christ Jesus our Lord" (Ephesians 3:11).

Immutable

As a part of God's immutability, His foreknowledge and foreordaining of events is done so without remorse, regret, or without change. Passages within the Scripture that mention God regretting or being remorseful are done so for purposes of human identification or mentioned in a way that can be

---

[95] Ibid, 311.

considered anthropomorphic in nature. Augustine best explains this by writing, "God wills not one thing now and another anon; but once and at once and always, he wills all things that he wills; not again and again, nor now this, now that; nor wills afterward what before he willed not, nor wills not before he willed; because such a will is mutable; and no mutable thing is eternal" (*Confessions* 12.15). Because divine thoughts are connected to the divine nature and essence, as the nature is eternal, so is the thought. We discover then, as Shedd writes, "The divine decree is the necessary condition of divine foreknowledge. If God does not first decide what shall come to pass, he cannot know what will come to pass. An event must be made certain before it can be known as a certain event."[96]

* * * * *

Considerations of the Divine Decree

Conflict with Free Will

Detractors of the divine decree point to a conflict between God's foreknowledge, or decree of an event

---

[96] Ibid, 313.

with man's free will in performing or acting out the actual event. The question is asked, how can man be free to do what he wants if God already preordained and knows of the event prior to creation? There is no conflict however, with the idea that an event may be certain to God yet uncertain to man. As God's nature is eternal, meaning His mind is infinite, He does by nature hold all things in His mind simultaneously without sequence. The difference for man is he holds finite knowledge and subsequently has difficulty comprehending the relationship between free will and the divine decree. God may know and understand that a certain man at a certain time, in a certain place, may do a certain thing, but God's sheer knowledge of the event does not necessarily negate the free will of the man's action.

Efficacious and Permissive

God's decrees are distributed between two classifications. Efficacious decrees set into motion or govern a happening, meaning that God is effective in getting the job done regarding His will and desires. For instance, the universe is set into motion by God and is sustained by God; "*He made a decree for the rain and a way for the lightning of the thunder*" (Job 28:26). God's foreknowledge of the workings, nature, and timing of the universe, and the substance contained within, was set prior to its creation.

The permissive decrees relate to sin and God's allowance of an action even though He does not endorse the action. Theologians refer to this as the permissive will of God regarding humanity. As creatures with free will, God allows man the freedom to choose, yet this does not equate to the idea that God approves or supports every choice man makes. This does bring a question, does God, as being sovereign, bear responsibility for sin or the creation of it? Shedd writes, "In creating man holy and giving him plenary power to persevere in holiness, God has done all that equity requires in reference to the prevention of sin in a moral agent." [97]

Predestination

As the divine decree relates to persons and not material items, it is said that God predestines persons

---

[97] William G.T. Shedd, *Dogmatic Theology*, (Phillipsburg, NJ: Reformed Publishing Company, 2003), 321.

and moral agents. Shedd comments, "God decreed rather than predestinated the existence of the material universe. Again a decree relates to a thing or fact; predestination to a person. Sin is decreed; the sinner is predestinated."[98] Paul writes, *"For those whom he foreknew he also predestined to be conformed to the image of his Son"* (Romans 8:29). Numerous supporting texts throughout Scripture illuminate this same thought. The deep question regarding this portion of the divine decree rests in God's knowing or God's favoring regarding specific human persons. It is important to know that God is within His power and nature to preordain all men to know Him and come into right relationship with Him. It is additionally within God's power and essence, as the Creator of the universe, to select from all humanity those whom He chooses for His own purpose. It seems to me, the former outweighs the later.

Election & Reprobation

Within the decree of predestination, we find the two decrees of election and reprobation. It is said that God gives to those who are predestined a

---

[98] Ibid, 324.

measure of grace to keep one from apostasy. The special measure of grace is not of man's good works or deeds, but rather from God's compassion for man and God's desire for man to remain holy and in right relationship with his Creator. Two additional concepts regarding election are irresistible grace and unconditional favor. On the converse of election stands reprobation. Shedd writes, "Reprobation is the antithesis to election and necessarily follow from it. If God does not elect a person, he rejects him."[99] This is a harsh saying indeed.

Some who hold to the doctrine of election, in the sense that God preordains certain persons for eternal life and not others, do not have the luxury of letting go of this harsh reverse reality. Shedd concludes, "Whoever holds the doctrine of election must hold the antithetic doctrine of reprobation." [100] Theologians of this position do hold that God gives common grace to all men, but irresistible grace is only for the elect. Again, it seems to me, Shedd and those holding this theological position are ahead of

---

[99] Ibid, 333.
[100] Ibid, 333.

their skis on this point. In sum, as much more can be discussed, for further study, the two main classifications of theological debate regarding this topic are the Arminian and Calvinistic points of view.

* * * * *

Open Theism & Divine Foreknowledge

In the book *Divine Foreknowledge*, Gregory Boyd argues for the defense of Open Theism. This view purports that although God is Omniscient, He does not necessarily know all future events. Boyd argues, "It holds that the reality that God perfectly knows not only excludes some possibilities as what might have been, but also includes other possibilities as what might be." [101] He continues in reference to God's reality that it "is composed of both settled and open aspects." [102] Boyd lays out his argument for his "openness view of creation" [103] with a biblical exegesis of both the classical view of God's foreknowledge and a scriptural motif outlining six

---

[101] Gregory A. Boyd, *Divine Foreknowledge* (Downers Grove, IL; InterVarsity Press, 2001), 14.
[102] Ibid. 14.
[103] Ibid. 14.

aspects illustrating the future as being partially open to God's foreknowledge. Boyd examines the classical view of God's foreknowledge, but holds the position that even though God's sovereign control of all of human history is clearly depicted in Scripture, it does not necessarily point to the fact, "that the future is exhaustively settled and known by god."[104]

Further Support For His View

He surveys additional biblical texts in which God asks questions about the future, regrets decisions, changes His mind, confronts the unexpected, expresses frustration, speaks in conditional terms, and tests people to know their character. Boyd declares an Open Theism understanding "makes better sense out of the whole of Scripture than alternative views."[105] Additionally, he opines there are pragmatic and theological advantages. Some of which are, clarifying why some individuals cause suffering, constructing a better understanding with recent advancements in science, and inspiring the benefits of prayer. Boyd concludes his remarks by

---

[104] Ibid. 15.
[105] Ibid. 47.

emphasizing that the classical view of God's foreknowledge "should be modified and expanded to include possibilities rather than limiting God's foreknowledge to settled facts."[106] He does grant on the inverse however, "that traditional concepts should not be revised without lengthy and prayerful process of discernment."[107] This is a statement to which we both agree.

God's Omniscience

Boyd's view of Open Theism, it seems to me, deteriorates divine omniscience and is deficient of a full view of Scripture. The standard definition of omniscience holds "that if future contingent propositions or counterfactuals of creaturely freedom are true, then they must be known by God."[108] Boyd affirms divine omniscience but yet denies that God is aware of all future contingents and counterfactuals. Boyd must conclude then, that all such propositions are not true. However, the problem is if those propositions are true, then God would be aware and

---

[106] Ibid. 47.
[107] Ibid. 47.
[108] William Lane Craig, *Divine Foreknowledge* (Downers Grove, IL; InterVarsity Press, 2001), 55.

Boyd's view "undermines divine omniscience."[109] Additionally, divine omniscience requires that God hold no false beliefs. Under Boyd's view, God's disappointment, regret, and expectation would be a false belief that God holds and consequently serves to distort divine omniscience.

Anthropomorphic Misunderstanding

Lastly, Boyd is lacking a proper view of scripture evolving from an incorrect focus on the anthropomorphic descriptions of God. Such descriptions of God as having arms and legs, seeing, hearing, or striking are not literal images. William Lane Craig points out, "Contrary to Boyd, we have every reason to be suspicious of a literal interpretation of passages that portray God as finite or limited." [110] Another problem with Boyd's hermeneutics is found in his emphasis of what could be called "dialogue"[111] scripture as opposed to "all things" scripture. Open Theism emphasizes the individual dialogue or personal descriptive verses of

---

[109] Ibid. 55.
[110] Ibid. 59.
[111] Paul Helm, *Divine Foreknowledge* (Downers Grove, IL; InterVarsity Press, 2001), 62.

God over the classical theism universal or "all things" verses that describe God's relation to humanity in a big picture format instead of individual or personal forms. Boyd interprets dialogue scripture literally. Proper hermeneutics requires an identical literal interpretation for "all things" scripture as well. Therefore, Open Theism seems to be an underdeveloped view that needs additional thought and work.

CHAPTER SEVEN

Creation

God & Time

Timeless and Omnitemporal

William Lane Craig, as a contributing author of *God & Time - Four Views*, offers a "hybrid view of divine eternity *that* is certainly curious."[112] Biblical writers reveal God in a manner that is both interactive with humanity and declarative as "the high and lofty one who inhabits eternity" (Isaiah 57:15). In light of these two perspectives, how should God's relation to time and eternity be viewed? An ardent reader of Scripture will quickly ascertain that the nature of God in eternity and His relationship to time is slightly ambiguous. Craig supports the view that God is both

---

[112] William Lane Craig, *God & Time, Four Views* (Downers Grove, IL; InterVarsity Press, 2001), 186.

Timeless and Omnitemporal. Omnitemporal means God exists at every time that ever exists.

Craig first questions divine timelessness. Medieval theologian Boethius wrote, "Whatever includes and possesses the whole fullness of interminable life at once and is such that nothing future is absent from it and nothing past has flowed away, this is rightly judged to be eternal."[113] Brian Leftow supports the idea of divine timelessness on the claim that God, as a most perfect being would be in conflict with a temporal life. Craig counters this argument, "Timeless life may not be the most perfect mode of existence of a perfect person."[114] He additionally points out that because God is personal, "the idea of a timeless person is incoherent and therefore God must be temporal."[115] Craig then turns his attention to focus on two supporting ideas.

Timeless San Creation

First, God's relationship to time is that He is timeless sans creation, meaning that God existed

---

[113] Ibid. 132.
[114] Ibid. 140.
[115] Ibid. 137.

alone without the universe. There is not a prior to or before the creation event. God simply existed in a state without time. This, according to Craig, allows God to be "timeless without creation."[116] For the theist, having a sufficient doctrine of *creation ex nihilo* is paramount to holding a coherent theological viewpoint. Craig reasons this doctrine affirms "God brought the universe into being out of nothing at some point in the finite past and that he thereafter sustains it in being moment by moment."[117] Craig goes on to explore the ideas of amorphous time and the doctrine of metric conventionalism in respect to time as supported by a number of philosophers of Oxford University. "God existing alone without the universe would exist in an amorphous time before the beginning of divisible time as we know it."[118] He concedes that the conclusion of God being timeless without the universe and temporal with the universe "is startling and not a little odd."[119] Nonetheless, he firmly holds this is the most coherent and plausible explanation.

---

[116] Ibid. 160.
[117] Ibid. 161.
[118] Ibid. 157.
[119] Ibid. 156.

Dynamic Theory of Time

Secondly, Craig holds to the dynamic theory of time as opposed to a static theory of time. He explores that after the creation event, our universe became a tensed universe not *tenseless*. Supporters of the static theory hold that every event is now and there are no true past or future tense(s). If the universe were tenseless, then God would not be temporal as Craig holds. This debate is often described as the A theory or B theory of time. Craig points out that "almost no defender of divine timelessness has taken this route."[120] Moreover, due to difficult philosophical and theological objections concerning the static theory, he prefers to "cast his lot with the dynamic theory."[121]

Time Marching Universe

Responses from Padgett and Wolterstorff seem supportive of Craig's position. Helm, holding to a B theory of time did offer a thoughtful response to Craig's position. Nonetheless, I would tend to side with Craig on this issue and support a dynamic theory

---

[120] Ibid. 152.
[121] Ibid. 152.

of time. If our universe is composed of events 'prior' to and 'after' all other events as we experience, then it holds that we live in a 'time marching' universe. If God, as a personal agent, interacts with His creatures in this 'time marching' universe, then He by nature would become temporal at the point of creation, due to those interactions. I am inclined to support Craig's perspective of God being both Timeless and Omnitemporal. This perspective is the 'best account' of scripture, experience, and science.

*****

A Day-Age View of Creation

A major point of concern among theologians, church leaders, and layman alike is the discussion of the age of the earth, including the age of the universe. The discussion tends to illicit decidedly passionate reactions from many within the Christian community. Putting reactions aside, what does the Scripture say regarding this important topic? First however, we say it is important on account of modern scientific observations pointing rather clearly to a conclusion that we live in an old universe. One may argue, "Old" compared to what? For the purpose of this discussion, "old" is in comparison to a Young Earth Creationist's view of the universe being under 10,000 years old. The importance of this discussion rests in the obvious conflict between these two differing points of view. Expected reasoning dictates we cannot live in an old and young universe simultaneously.

What is the Day-Age View?

The day-age view is built "upon the conviction that we can trust God's revelation as truth in both the words of the Bible and the works of creation, including the entire physical universe." [122] It is important to note this view holds to a literal translation of the Bible in every sense of the word, not only in the Genesis creation accounts, but in all biblical creation descriptions as well. Dr. Hugh Ross writes, "Our day-age interpretation treats the creation days literally as six sequential, long periods of time. Integrating biblical and scientific data, we assert that the physical creation events reported in Genesis appear in correct sequence and in scientifically

---

[122] David G. Hagopian, *The Genesis Debate: Three Views on the Days of Creation* (Mission Viejo, CA; Crux Press, Inc., 2001), 123.

defensible terms."[123] Additionally, Ross points out this views holds all humanity, *homo sapiens*, are direct decedents of Adam and Eve and appeared no longer than a "few tens of thousands of years ago."[124]

Yom = Day

Much of the dialogue regarding these two views rests on small but powerful Hebrew word, *yom*. One challenge when interpreting the Bible is a difference in vocabulary between biblical Hebrew and modern English. For example, historical Hebrew contained "under 3,100 words (not including proper nouns), English words number over 4,000,000." [125] This brings a challenge to the conversation when interpreting the word *yom*, which means day. We may not always know, at first reading, what the author intended to communicate. However, what we do know is, "Hebrew nouns have multiple literal definitions."[126]

This should not seem strange to us as the word *day* may mean more than one thing in modern-day

---

[123] Ibid, 123.
[124] Ibid, 124.
[125] Ibid, 125.
[126] Ibid, 125.

English as well, the play on words here intended. In Hebrew, writers often did the same thing. In most cases, with a much smaller vocabulary to work with, the word *yom* was used in various ways, thereby attaching diverse meanings to distinctive concepts. One important factor to point out is, "biblical Hebrew has no word other than *yom* to denote a long timespan."[127] Additionally, the words *yom* and *yamin* are utilized throughout Scripture to expressly mean non-24 hour periods of time or more specifically long periods of time.

New or Old Debate?

From what information can be gathered from the earliest of Church fathers' writings, it is not obvious that this current theological/cultural debate was even discussed with any sort of fervency. Ross writes, "Prior to the Nicene Council, the early Church fathers wrote two thousand pages of commentary on the Genesis creation days, yet did not devote a word to disparaging each other's viewpoints on the creation time scale. All these early scholars accepted that *yom* could mean 'a long time period.' The majority

[127] Ibid, 125.

explicitly taught that the Genesis creation days were extended time periods (something like a thousand years per *yom*)."[128]

Additionally, we find there is no evidence that any Ante-Nicene leaders endorsed the 24-hour viewpoint either. Interesting, Ross points out, "They wrote [this] long before astronomical, geological, and paleontological evidences for the antiquity of the universe, the earth, and life become available."[129] So, although we may find a rather big divide within this Christianized intermural debate, the evidence of a similar divide within Scripture or the early Church leaders cannot be found.

Summary

It seems to me that those holding to a 24-hour view do so with reasons attached to their understanding of the word *yom,* meaning one single day. Yet within that mindset, they are limiting their interpretation to only one of a few options. It seems early Christians held a more open view since there

---

[128] Ibid, 126.
[129] Ibid, 126.

was no data either way to make an informed decision on the matter. However, as scientific data and solid research has shown clear support for an old universe, there simply is no biblical mandate to hold to the perspective that our world is under 10,000 years old. Passion for biblical inerrancy is held by both viewpoints so the debate does not center on this argument. Furthermore, belief in miracles and God's right to morph or modify laws of nature at His will are again supported by both views, so the discussion does not find an anchor point here. Lastly, good people can disagree, and when we do, we can do so agreeably. If we, as Christians, are unable to do so, what hope do others have, who do not know Christ's will?

* * * * *

Testing the Day-Age Model

A Fascinating Thought

Two contributing factors to the benefit and trustworthiness of one's belief are in its accuracy of Scripture and truthfulness to known realities. For example, if I were to postulate that you, all matter, and I were created only 15 days ago would that belief fit known reality and Scriptural truths? Of course not, right? But, what if I argued that God can do anything, so therefore, why didn't He create a fully appearing human history and all living organisms 15 days ago complete with the appearance of an old or young universe that He allows us to debate its age? Furthermore, according to my postulation, God can do anything and to limit Him from doing this is to put him in a box constructed by human limitations.

Refuse The Rabbit Hole

What comes to the rescue from this type of "Alice in Wonderland" thinking? Good theology and solid philosophy. Good theology looks through the myriad of philosophical ideologies in the hopes of finding those two factors mentioned above, *accuracy of Scripture* and *truthfulness to known realities*. As human beings, created in the image of God, we utilize these two factors to gain a proper understanding of the world around us, and our place in it.

Four Models

In looking at potential creation models, we tend to observe four different concepts; naturalism, also known as Darwinian evolution, the 24-hour belief, the framework concept, and the day-age model. We find the day-age model to best fit our two criteria of Scripture and known reality. In contrast, Ross and Archer mention, "Darwinian evolution, chaos theory, and six consecutive 24-hour day creationism fail to predict and, in fact, contradict the growing body of data. The framework interpretation offers no model for life's history and, therefore, cannot be tested."[130] What are, at a minimum, two testable factors to support the day-age concept?

Fossil Record

If one were to pick up a modern-day science book, one would find the fossil record in the form of a tree. This Darwinian tree of life appears to show the first life in the root section of the tree and as the tree grows so does all life forms into more complex and supportive formats driven by the lower forms. The problem is, the fossil record does not show this format. Ross and Archer write, "What the growing database does show is that many life forms persisted

---

[130] David G. Hagopian, *The Genesis Debate: Three Views on the Days of Creation* (Mission Viejo, CA; Crux Press, Inc., 2001), 139.

through several millennia without significant morphological change, then became extinct."[131] This leads us to the conclusion there seems to be missing horizontal branches in the fossil record. To complicate the issue, we find after a long gap of time, some extinct or similar species reappear and the appearance arrives without any natural method to justify it. Ross and Archer explain, "This fossil pattern contradicts naturalism, but it precisely fits what the day-age creation model predicts. According to that model, God supernaturally introduced new species, sometimes with a little change, sometimes with significant change, replacing those that became extinct."[132]

One other interesting factor is a reversal of the Darwinian view. Simply put, modern-day evolutionary data show a reversal, of sort, in the tree of life. Ross and Archer write, "As time advances, fewer and fewer species remain on the earth, and the most advanced species show the fastest extinction rates. Naturalism has yet to offer a plausible

[131] Ibid, 139.
[132] Ibid, 139.

117

explanation for this change." [133] This type of 'reversal' however fits perfecting into the day-age theory. From the beginning of life, God has created and recreated many times over. During the many epochs of time since the foundations of our planet, the fossil record shows a creator actively changing, modifying, or replacing differing species until he creates human beings, *homo sapiens*, in his own image. According to the biblical account, on the sixth day, God's creation was complete. God now is in a period of creation rest on day Seven. Ross and Archer conclude, "Before Adam and Eve, the history of life was shaped predominantly by supernatural interventions."[134]

A Recent Origin of Humanity

According to the day-age model, biblical genealogies and other Scriptural factors point to a recent origin of humanity. By most standards, "Conservative estimates among biblical scholars for the creation of Adam and Eve range from about 10,000 to 60,000 year ago." [135] Remarkably, two

---

[133] Ibid, 140.
[134] Ibid, 140.
[135] Ibid, 141.

fascinating advancements in molecular biology reveal support for this date range. The ability to study humanity's "genetic clock" through mitochondrial DNA and Y-chromosomes is captivating to say the least. Ross and Archer write, "Today's best understanding of this DNA research data places the first woman at about 50,000 years ago and the most recent common ancestor of men (which would be Noah, rather than Adam, according to the biblical record) at 37,000-49,000) years ago."[136] Even recent studies of Neanderthals, gorillas, orangutans, and chimpanzees "demonstrate that these different species cannot have arisen naturally from a common ancestor.

Yet again, the biblical account fits the accumulating data."[137] The dating of land bridges to Australia and the Americas sometime between 11,000-30,000 years ago supports a recent origin and migration of humanity. Additionally, the most "ancient remnant of advance art has been dated as 32,000 years old."[138] Lastly, artifacts of religious

---

[136] Ibid, 141.
[137] Ibid, 142.
[138] Ibid, 142

expression also date to 8,000-24,000 years ago. Ross and Archer conclude, "All these finding support the biblical day-age creation scenario and the subsequent chapters of Genesis as well."[139]

---

[139] Ibid, 142.

CHAPTER EIGHT

Providence & Miracles

Providence

When we speak of providence concerning God and His relationship with creation, we mean to say that God is the one being who sustains all things and governs all things. Sustain can best be described as preservation. It would be incorrect and illogical for that which was created *ex nihilo* to be self-sustaining. If it were true that all matter and beings within this created order sustained itself, the question would arise; from where does, or where would, this creation from nothing derives its power to function and exist? The preservation of all creation rests in God's sustaining power. Thus God could at His command simply cease to uphold this creation, and at that moment all would be destroyed. This is a sobering thought for us to consider as the Scripture declares, "He upholds the universe by the word of his power" (Hebrews 1:3).

What Type of Preservation

It is important to also note that God's preservation of His creation, especially in relation to humanity, "is more than merely imparting to matter certain properties and placing it under certain invariable laws. This is the deistical view of providence."[140] This view holds that God is not personally involved with his creation. God is nothing more than a watchmaker who after creating a beautiful watch, wound it up and walked away to leave the watch ticking on its own power. This view however does not fit the biblical view of divine providence. Likewise, pantheism, which "allows no secondary substance and no second cause,"[141] does not fit a proper biblical understanding.

Pantheism holds the idea that God is the only substance in the universe and the only agent. But we know from Scripture, "preservation is the immediate

---

[140] William G.T. Shedd, *Dogmatic Theology*, (Phillipsburg, NJ: Reformed Publishing Company, 2003), 412.

[141] Ibid, 412.

operation of God as a distinct and different being upon, in, and with the creature as a different and distinct being and always in accordance with the nature of the creature."[142] Additionally, as a properly basic belief, we exist as exclusive and separate entities apart from God and as human creatures, we know we possess individuality, free will, and an autonomous soul.

God works in connection with His creatures in a similar fashion as the soul of man works with the body. This is an incomplete illustration but does serve as a "best illustration of the mode in which God operates in providence."[143] We find this declaration in Acts 17:28, "In him we live and move and have our being." God's activity in relation to providence is connected to the following areas:

1. Physical Nature, *"You cause the grass to grow for the livestock and plants for man to cultivate."* (Psalm 104:14)

---

[142] Ibid, 413.
[143] Ibid, 413.

2. Animal Creation, "*Look at the birds of the air: they neither sow nor reap nor gather into barns, and yet your heavenly Father feeds them.*" (Matthew 6:26)

3. Human History, "*He changes times and seasons; he removes kings and sets up kings*" (Daniel 2:21).

4. Individual Life, "*The heart of man plans his ways, but the Lord establishes his steps*" (Proverb 16:9).

5. Particulars & Universals, "*Even the hairs of your head are all numbered*" (Luke 12:7).

6. Free Actions of Men, "*For it is God who works in you, both to will and to work for his good pleasure*" (Philippians 2:13).

7. Sinful Action of Men, "*For God has consigned all to disobedience, that he may have mercy on all*" (Romans 11:32).

Governance

The providence of God is additionally seen through His governing of the affairs of man. God governs the affairs of man through His creation. He does so through both physical causes and through divine interaction with individual people. God may use the physical forces of the universe to impart His governance upon His creation. Additionally, God is free to impart His sustenance upon mankind. God imparts upon the human soul, through the Holy Spirit "influence, instruction, persuasion, and example."[144] God thus influences His divine plan through His people. Although man is free to participate in the plan of God, God is not obligated to use man nor does He make His plan contingent upon man to do so. God will accomplish His plan and through providence, sustain His plan until His plan for this present creation is complete.

* * * * *

Miracles

Superseding Law

In the working out of God's government upon earth, God will at His own pleasure utilize the miraculous. A few explanations are necessary. The miraculous is not the idea of special and unordinary events superseding natural law by the use of a greater

---

[144] Ibid, 415.

or different unknown natural law; thereby allowing the materialist to deny the miraculous in the hope science will discover these currently unknown natural laws to explain the miraculous events we experience as human begins. If this were true, as the materialist holds, it would result in the operation of two conflicting natural forces within our universe. If there were two conflicting natural laws, we would have no knowledge of the lesser law on account of the greater law's continual higher weight over the lesser law. Otherwise, we would experience a continual state of equilibrium if both laws carried equal power, thus resulting in no concept of miracle at all and leaving us with an illogical conclusion as to the driving force behind the experience of miracles.

Suspension of Law

It would be proper to say that a miracle is from a different source outside of this universe and is caused by God's divine power or agency upon His creation. We can gain an understanding by seeing the miracle as "a suspension of a law of nature in a particular instance" [145] and not "a violation of the laws of

---

[145] William G.T. Shedd, *Dogmatic Theology*, (Phillipsburg, NJ: Reformed Publishing Company, 2003), 419.

nature."[146] It is additionally important to note that a simple suspension of a law of nature is not adequate to reason for the miracle alone. A miracle needs an impartation of power or unction from the divine source. Without such, Shedd writes, "Christ, by virtue of the control which he had over natural law, might have arrested the process of decomposition, and yet Lazarus would not have come forth from the tomb, any more than he would if he had been embalmed or petrified ... there must have been the exertion of a positively reanimating power."[147]

Natural to God

Miracles, although unnatural to man, are not unnatural to God. When we see a miracle in our universe, we catch a glimpse of what is natural to God in heaven. Shedd also points out, "Miracles are natural to a personal deity, but unnatural and impossible to an impersonal." [148] If God were impersonal as the deist holds, He would have no compulsion to interact with His creation since all the parameters and directives would have been created

---

[146] Ibid, 419.
[147] Ibid, 419.
[148] Ibid, 417.

and laid down at the foundations of the world. God would then be free to walk away from man and watch from a distance the working out of the predetermined actions of all creation. Because we see miracles and divine intervention in the affairs of man, we can conclude God is personal and takes an interest in man and His purposes for us. Theologians argue that we should expect to see miracles from God. It would be natural to conclude that personality is expressed through interaction driven by showing empathy for what the person cares for. In relation to God and His divine personhood, we can expect to see love and care for His creation produce interaction with us. In many of those interactions, God may chose and does choose to utilize His divine power to show us a glimpse of His nature while in that moment showing us what we have come to name the miraculous.

* * * * *

Miracles – Are they Possible

An Intriguing Notion

"It's a miracle," a comment we frequently hear from maternity wards to college graduations. When a spectacular or meaningful event takes place in life, we celebrate by declaring its singularity. There is nothing intrinsically wrong or unscientific in this celebration. However, looking deeper into the authenticity of the extraordinary, most would conclude these types of events are not truly miraculous. It does imply a fascinating question however, are miracles possible?

Hume's Argument

The answer is important to a common objection regarding the resurrection of Jesus Christ. If miracles are possible, then the events as told by the biblical texts could be correct. However, according to eighteenth century philosopher Dave Hume, miracles are impossible, "I flatter myself that I have discovered an argument...which, if just, will, with the wise and learned, be an everlasting check to all kinds of superstitious delusion, and consequently will be useful as long as the world endures."[149] His viewpoint is famously described as an argument against the miraculous and if his viewpoint is correct,

---

[149] Norman Geisler, *"Miracles and Modern Scientific Thought"* (Blog), Quoting David Hume, *An Inquiry Concerning Human Understanding*, ed. C. W. Hendel (New York: Bobbs-Merrill, 1955), 10.1.118, accessed, March 20, 2017, http://www.leaderu.com/truth/1truth19.html.

then Christianity is dead in its tracks. Nonetheless, Hume's logic is flawed and dated. Consequently, it is reasonable to conclude that miracles are not only possible but also supported by logic and newly developed scientific facts.

Outside Agency

Miracles suggest events that break, intervene, modify, or add to the natural laws of the universe. These are events that cannot be explained by natural means and seem to indicate an agency or mechanism outside natural laws. We have come to label these events as supernatural, or outside of the natural world. For an event to be truly miraculous, it would have to be compelled by a source outside to what we normally observe. As an example, Jesus walking on water would qualify as a miracle. He either was breaking a known law of gravity by floating on the surface of the water or the known laws of buoyancy were violated because His mass was not properly displacing the amount of water equal to His body mass. Either way, according to the eyewitness accounts, a miraculous event took place on the Sea of Galilee that day.

When the skeptic says miracles are impossible, this becomes an argument from possibility. To say something is impossible means all other options have been explored and none of those possibilities are available to provide an acceptable answer. Is it truly impossible that an outside mechanism or agency can and does interact with the known laws of the universe? Let's explore the possibility.

Natural or Supernatural?

From the period of the enlightenment, modern man has developed a perspective that we live in a closed system. Call it a fishbowl if you will. Everything we know of and experience from all levels simply resides inside our fishbowl. For someone to suggest there is something outside of this system is a tough pill to swallow for the materialist. From where does the materialist gain this assessment? He gains this viewpoint from inside the fishbowl. There is a logical inconsistency from this perspective.

It's actually entirely impossible for those inside the closed system to ever truly know, with one

133

hundred percent certainty, that there is nothing outside the system that could and can act as a mechanism or agency on the closed system. To say otherwise is simply avoiding the potential for all possible answers. The very fact that the human mind can fathom the idea of an '*outside*' to our universe suggests its possibility and more importantly its probability.

What Hume did not know is that our universe is not a completely closed system. It is not as C.S. Lewis describes, "self-existent."[150] At least, it's not as Big Bang Cosmology has described it. We now know our universe had a beginning and the cause of that beginning must have been something outside of the natural laws contained inside the universe. It is no fault of Hume or earlier philosophers to not have seen this viewpoint; however, in today's world, based upon Cosmology, it would be unreasonable to hold to a view that our universe is an entirely closed system. It is therefore possible that the supernatural, or that which would be considered outside of the natural,

---

[150] C.S. Lewis, *The Complete C.S. Lewis Signature Classics*, (New York, NY: Harper One Publishers, 2002) 449.

could intersect with our natural laws and either break, intervene, modify, add or otherwise confound us.

Quantum Mechanics

Another possibility that supports the idea that miracles are possible is the emergence of quantum mechanics over the past one hundred years. Quantum mechanics has radically changed the way in which physicists view the world. From the very smallest of levels, particles and waveforms behave in very non-conforming ways.

This was a surprise to physicists and scientists from all fields. C.S. Lewis describes this quantum world as sub-natural and not super-natural. Yet he concludes, "There is apparently something outside her, the Subnatural; it is indeed from this Subnatural that all events and all 'bodies' are, as it were, fed into her. And clearly if she thus has a backdoor opening on the Subnatural, it is quite on the cards that she may also have a front door opening on the Supernatural—and events might be fed into her at that door too."[151]

---

[151] Ibid, 312.

Heisenberg Uncertainty Principle

A popular objection to this line of thinking is that the universe does not include entities, which are incomprehensible or isolated from science and reason. "Again, quantum mechanics demolishes this idea. The Heisenberg Uncertainty principle is a good, popular response to this objection since it explicitly states that some realities like the simultaneous position and momentum of a particle are unknowable. More generally, in quantum mechanics, the fundamental object is the wave-function, which is essentially inaccessible to measurement." [152] Therefore, according to quantum mechanics, ultimate reality is not always observable.

The natural laws handed down from the period of the Enlightenment and Age of Reason no longer hold true in the strictest sense of the word. The laws of physics, which were once ironclad, no longer deal with certainties. Through quantum mechanics, scientific discovery has found a world of probabilities that has replaced certainties. Since probabilities are

---

[152] Neil Shenvi, *Quantum mechanics and materialism* (Blog), accessed March 20, 2017, http://www.shenvi.org/Essays/QuantumMechanics.htm.

the driving force on the quantum level, it would be entirely possible that a miraculous event could happen, thus making the proposition of miracles being possible, well…possible.

Summary

To summarize, the Christian does not need to approach the objection to miracles from the basic argument that there is a God, and therefore He can intervene if He wants. The arguments from personal experience, eyewitness accounts, and the reasonableness of God's existence are all valid ideas. However, the materialist will fight those arguments tooth and nail. Approaching this discussion from a philosophical and scientific perspective reinforces the position that miracles are possible from a different way.

About the Author

Having served in pastoral ministry positions for 17 years and having served at the executive level of two Fortune 500 companies for 14 years, T.K. Anderson is a seasoned leader in both the affairs of business and Christian ministries.

He is the author of two books, *Pocket Theology: Getting God* and *Faith Jump Vol. 1.0*, has spoken to tens of thousands of people in numerous countries around the globe, earned a Bachelor's degree in Theological Studies from North Central University and a Master's degree in Christian Apologetics from Biola University.

He is the founder of Faithjump.com and currently serves as Pastor of The Social Media Church (TSMchurch.com), and President of the National Institute of Apologetics.

Bibliography

- Boyd, Gregory A., *Divine Foreknowledge* (Downers Grove, IL: InterVarsity Press, 2001)

- Craig, William Lane, "A Nominalist Perspective on God and Abstract Objects," *Philosophia Christi* 13 (2011)

- Craig, William Lane, *God & Time, Four Views* (Downers Grove, IL: InterVarsity Press, 2001)

- Flew, Antony with Varghese, Ray Abraham, *There Is a God* (San Francisco, CA: HarperOne, 2007)

- Groothuis, Douglas, *Christian Apologetics A Comprehensive Case for Biblical Faith* (Downers Grove, Il: InterVarsity Press, 2011)

- Hagopian, David G., *The Genesis Debate: Three Views on the Days of Creation* (Mission Viejo, CA: Crux Press, Inc., 2001)

- Hume, David, *"To John Stewart," Letter 91*, ed. J.Y.T. Greig (Oxford, Eng; Clarendon, 1932)

- Lewis, C.S., *The Complete C.S. Lewis Signature Classics* (New York, NY: Harper One Publishers, 2002)

- Moreland, J.P. Moreland & Craig, William Lane, *Philosophical Foundations for a Christian Worldview* (Downers Grove, Il: InterVarsity Press, 2003)
- Shedd, William G.T., *Dogmatic Theology* (Phillipsburg, NJ: Reformed Publishing Company, 2003)